ADOBE

PHOTOSHOP 2025

USER GUIDE

The Complete Beginner-to-Expert Manual to
Mastering Photo Editing with Updated Tools,
Shortcuts, and Creative Techniques

ALBERT F. JOHNSON

DISCLAIMER

This guide is an independent publication and is not affiliated with or endorsed by Adobe Inc. "Adobe" and "Photoshop" are trademarks of Adobe Inc.

The content is for educational purposes only. While every effort has been made to ensure accuracy, features may change with software updates. Users should refer to Adobe's official documentation for the latest information.

The author and publisher are not liable for any outcomes resulting from the use of this guide.

TABLE OF CONTENT

Introduction

From Overwhelm to Mastery –
Your Journey Starts Here

The screen was glowing.

Dozens of tiny icons sat at the top, strange toolbars hugged every corner, and a blank canvas stretched out in the center like a challenge waiting to be solved. *"What does this button even do?"* they whispered to themselves, clicking cautiously... only to undo. Undo again. Close the program. And walk away.

That's how it begins for most people. Not with a burst of creativity—but with a quiet kind of defeat.

If you're anything like the countless aspiring creators who've opened Adobe Photoshop for the first time—hoping to design something amazing—you've probably felt that same mix of excitement and confusion. You've watched tutorials that moved too fast, read guides that talked over your head, or followed steps that made you feel like you were missing some invisible lesson everyone else got.

You're not alone.

Behind every brilliant digital artist, every sharp flyer, every retouched photo you admire, there's a story that started with frustration. And chances are, nobody ever told you that learning Photoshop wasn't about mastering *everything*—it's about knowing the *right* things, in the *right* order, with the *right guidance*.

That's what this book is about.

Not drowning you in jargon. Not throwing all 70+ tools at you at once. Not assuming you already know what "clipping mask" or "smart object" means. This guide is here to be your *companion*, your *translator*, and your *cheerleader* as you step into the world of Photoshop 2025—whether it's for the first time or the tenth time.

In this guide, you'll find:

- **Real-world tasks** broken down step-by-step
- **Screenshots and visual aids** that show *exactly* what to do

- **Clear explanations** of tools, features, and when to use them
- **Creative tips and design principles** that help you think like a pro
- And above all, the **confidence** to open Photoshop and finally say: *"I've got this."*

You don't need talent.

You don't need expensive classes.

You just need the right roadmap.

Whether you're a student, small business owner, hobbyist, or creative professional, this book was written for *you.* By the time you finish it, Photoshop won't feel like a foreign language anymore. It'll feel like a tool you *own*—and one you can use to bring your wildest ideas to life.

Let's get started.

Let's turn that frustration into power.

Who This Book is For

Whether you're opening Photoshop for the first time or you've tried to learn it in the past but felt overwhelmed, this book was designed with *you* in mind.

It's for:

- **Beginners** who want to learn Photoshop from the ground up—without getting lost in the complexity.
- **Photographers and digital artists** looking to polish their images, retouch with precision, and finally understand the tools they've been guessing through.

- **Students and design learners** who need a structured, visual guide to complement their courses.
- **Entrepreneurs, marketers, and content creators** who want to create stunning graphics, banners, and visuals for their brands—without relying on others.
- **Hobbyists and creatives** who just want to *have fun* with Photoshop—making art, memes, or social media content that pops.

If you've ever said to yourself, *"I wish someone could just show me what to do, clearly and step-by-step,"*—this book is exactly that.

What's New in Adobe Photoshop 2025

Photoshop 2025 introduces a bold leap forward—built with more intelligence, speed, and creative power than ever before. Here are some of the standout new features you'll discover in this edition:

- **Enhanced AI Tools**: From smarter selections to next-gen *Generative Fill*, Photoshop's artificial intelligence can now predict, complete, and enhance your work with just a few clicks.

- **Real-Time Object Removal**: No more struggling with the clone tool—Photoshop 2025 allows near-instant removal of people, power lines, or objects, with stunning accuracy.

- **Brush & Tool Customization Panel**: An improved, drag-and-drop panel makes organizing your favorite brushes and tools smoother than ever.

- **Neural Filters Upgrade**: Even more creative control over skin smoothing, color grading, and facial adjustments—with better results and faster performance.

- **Live Collaboration Features**: Work on the same file in real time with others, making Photoshop a more dynamic, team-friendly experience.

- **Faster Performance & GPU Optimization**: Speed improvements across all devices, especially for larger files and multi-layer projects.

- **Improved Mobile/Cloud Integration**: Start on desktop, tweak on tablet, finish in the cloud—Photoshop 2025 brings tighter cross-platform functionality.

Each of these features will be explored in this guide with practical, real-world applications, so you're not just reading about what's new—you're actually using it.

System Requirements and Installation Guide

Before diving into your creative journey, let's make sure your system is ready to run Photoshop 2025 smoothly. Adobe has raised the bar a little with this release, especially to support the latest AI-driven features.

☑ **Minimum System Requirements:**

- **Operating System**: Windows 11 (64-bit) or macOS Monterey (12.0) and above
- **Processor**: Intel® or AMD processor with 64-bit support; 2 GHz or faster processor
- **RAM**: 8 GB (16 GB recommended for best performance)
- **Graphics Card**: GPU with DirectX 12 support (2 GB VRAM minimum, 4 GB recommended)
- **Hard Drive**: 10 GB of available space; SSD recommended
- **Display**: 1280 x 800 display (1920 x 1080 or higher preferred)
- **Internet**: Required for software activation and access to Adobe Creative Cloud features

Installation Steps:

1. **Create or Sign In to Adobe Account**

   Visit adobe.com, click "Sign In," or create a free account if you don't have one.

2. **Choose a Subscription Plan**

   Select the plan that suits your needs. (Photoshop is available as a standalone app or part of the Adobe Creative Cloud suite.)

3. **Download Adobe Creative Cloud Desktop App**

   This is the hub where you'll install and manage your Adobe applications.

4. **Install Photoshop 2025**

   Launch Creative Cloud, find Photoshop in the app list, and click "Install."

5. **Launch & Activate**

   Once installed, open Photoshop, sign

in with your Adobe ID, and you're ready to go.

⚠ **Tip:** Always check Adobe's website for the latest specs or updates—especially if you're using a newly released OS or hardware.

Chapter 1: Getting Started

Navigating the Photoshop Interface

When you first launch Adobe Photoshop 2025, the interface might feel a bit overwhelming. But once you understand the layout and purpose of each section, it becomes your creative playground.

✦ **The Home Screen**

Upon opening Photoshop, you'll see the **Home screen**, where you can:

- Create a new document
- Open recent files
- Access tutorials, templates, or Adobe resources

You can always return to the Home screen by clicking **File > Home** or using the home icon in the upper left.

✦ Main Interface Layout

Area	Description
Menu Bar	Located at the top; includes dropdown menus like File, Edit, Image, Layer, Type, Select, Filter, 3D, View, Window, and Help.
Toolbox (Tools Panel)	Usually on the left side; holds all the main tools like Move, Marquee, Brush, Eraser, etc. Hover over each to see tool tips.
Options Bar	Directly under the Menu Bar; changes depending on the selected tool, giving context-sensitive settings.
Panels and Workspaces	Found on the right side; includes Layers, Properties, Adjustments, Color, History, etc. You can customize and save your workspace.

Area	Description
Canvas	The main working area in the center where your image or design is displayed.
Status Bar	At the bottom; shows zoom level, color profile, and quick access settings.

Tip: Go to **Window > Workspace > Essentials (Default)** if your layout ever feels too chaotic.

Customizing Your Workspace

Photoshop gives you full control over how your interface looks and functions. Custom workspaces improve your workflow and reduce distractions.

✦ Choosing a Workspace

Photoshop offers pre-set workspaces tailored to different workflows:

- **Essentials** – The default layout
- **Photography** – Ideal for photo retouching
- **Graphic and Web** – Useful for layout design
- **Motion** – For timeline-based animation
- **3D** – If 3D editing is enabled on your device

Select via: **Window > Workspace > [Your Choice]**

✦ Rearranging Panels

- Drag any panel tab (e.g., Layers, Properties) to reposition it.
- Collapse panels by clicking the double arrows >> on the top right.
- Dock panels by dragging them to the edge of the screen.

✦ Saving a Custom Workspace

Once you've set things the way you like:

Go to **Window > Workspace > New Workspace**, give it a name, and save.

🔧 **Pro Tip**: Keep your Layers and History panels visible at all times—they're essential for nearly every project.

Understanding File Formats & Resolution

Before creating a new project, it's crucial to understand what file types to use and how resolution affects your work.

✦ Common Photoshop File Formats

Format	Description	Use Case
.PSD	Photoshop's native format; preserves	Best for ongoing projects

Format	Description	Use Case
	layers, effects, masks, etc.	
.JPEG / .JPG	Flattened image format; compressed	Web or social media sharing
.PNG	Supports transparency, lossless compression	Logos, graphics with no background
.TIFF	High-quality, supports layers	Printing, archiving
.PDF	Useful for print layouts	Exporting flyers, posters

✦ Understanding Resolution

- **DPI (Dots Per Inch)**: Used in print. Standard: **300 DPI**
- **PPI (Pixels Per Inch)**: Used on screens. Standard: **72 PPI**

⚠ Low resolution results in blurry prints. Always start with the correct dimensions for your target output (print or digital).

Setting Preferences

To make Photoshop more responsive to your workflow, tweak its settings.

Go to: **Edit (Windows) / Photoshop (Mac) > Preferences**

Some useful categories:

- **General**: Autosave, undo levels, export clipboard
- **Performance**: Adjust RAM usage, enable GPU acceleration
- **Tools**: Customize how brushes behave, show tool tips
- **Interface**: Switch between light/dark themes, scale UI

- **File Handling**: Set autosave intervals, default save locations

🛠 **Tip**: Enable "Legacy Undo" under Preferences > Performance if you prefer the classic multiple-undo system.

Chapter 2: Basic Tools & Functions

Photoshop's tool panel may look intimidating at first, but learning the basics unlocks nearly everything else you'll do. Each tool has a specific purpose, and when used together, they form the foundation of photo editing, digital painting, graphic design, and more.

Move, Marquee, Lasso, and Quick Selection Tools

Move Tool (V)

- **Function**: Moves selected elements (layers, text, images) around the canvas.
- **Key Features**:

- o Auto-Select: Allows you to click and move objects without manually selecting their layers.
- o Show Transform Controls: Lets you resize the selected element without switching tools.

💬 **Use Case**: Moving a logo to a new position on a flyer.

Marquee Tools (M)

- **Function**: Makes rectangular, elliptical, or single-row selections.
- **Types**:
  - o Rectangular Marquee
  - o Elliptical Marquee
  - o Single Row / Column

🧠 **Use Case**: Selecting a specific area of an image to apply a filter or adjustment.

Lasso Tools (L)

- **Function**: Allows for freehand and polygonal selections.
- **Types**:
  - Lasso: Freehand selection
  - Polygonal Lasso: Straight-edged selections
  - Magnetic Lasso: Snaps to edges based on contrast

💬 **Use Case**: Roughly cutting out a person or object from a photo.

Quick Selection Tool (W)

- **Function**: Selects areas based on similar color and texture.

- Drag over a region, and it expands the selection as you go.
- Works well with **Select and Mask** for refining edges.

Use Case: Quickly selecting the background to replace it with another.

Crop and Transform Tools

Crop Tool (C)

- **Function**: Cuts out portions of an image or changes canvas size.
- You can also straighten images using the angle tool within Crop.

Use Case: Cropping a photo to Instagram's square aspect ratio (1:1).

Transform Tools

- Accessed via **Edit > Free Transform** or shortcut **Ctrl + T (Cmd + T)**
- Allows you to:
  - Resize
  - Rotate
  - Skew
  - Flip
  - Warp

💬 **Use Case**: Resizing a photo to fit inside a poster layout or rotating a tilted image.

Brush, Eraser, and Gradient Tools

Brush Tool (B)

- **Function**: Paints color using custom shapes, hardness, and opacity.
- Ideal for digital painting, retouching, and masking.

💬 **Use Case**: Painting shadows or highlights onto a photo.

Eraser Tool (E)

- **Function**: Erases parts of an image or layer.
- Acts like a brush in reverse—can be soft, hard, or even textured.
- Erasing on a locked background converts it to a layer automatically.

💬 **Use Case**: Removing stray edges or cleaning up a digital sketch.

Gradient Tool (G)

- **Function**: Fills a selected area with a gradual blend of colors.
- You can customize:

- Direction (linear, radial, angle, reflected)
- Colors and stops
- Transparency

Use Case: Creating a smooth sky background or modern button effect.

Text and Shape Tools

Text Tool (T)

- **Function**: Adds editable text layers to your canvas.
- You can set:
  - Font type, size, color, alignment, spacing, and transformation.
- Supports paragraph and point text formats.

👄 **Use Case**: Adding a title to a flyer or a quote to a social media post.

Shape Tool (U)

- **Function**: Creates vector shapes— rectangles, ellipses, lines, polygons, and custom shapes.
- Each shape is a separate layer and can be resized without losing quality.

🧠 **Use Case**: Designing badges, icons, or buttons with clean edges.

Practice Exercises

These exercises are designed to help you reinforce what you've just learned in this chapter. Try completing each one step-by-step using a new or existing image in Photoshop.

🔧 Exercise 1: Rearranging a Photo Layout

Goal: Use the **Move Tool**

Open any image and duplicate the layer (Ctrl + J / Cmd + J).

Move the duplicate layer slightly off-center using the Move Tool.

Turn on "Show Transform Controls" and try resizing or rotating it.

☑ *What you've practiced:* Moving, duplicating, and transforming layers.

■ Exercise 2: Framing with the Marquee Tool

Goal: Use the **Rectangular Marquee Tool**

Create a new blank document.

Draw a rectangle with the Marquee Tool.

Fill it with a color (Edit > Fill or use the Paint Bucket).

Deselect (Ctrl + D / Cmd + D) and create another shape next to it.

☑ *What you've practiced:* Making and filling selections.

✂ Exercise 3: Cutting with Lasso Tools

Goal: Use **Lasso and Magnetic Lasso Tools**

Open an image with a distinct object (like a person or item).

Use the Lasso Tool to manually draw around the object.

Try the Magnetic Lasso to snap along edges.

Press Delete or Mask it out.

☑ *What you've practiced:* Manual and edge-aware selections.

🎯 Exercise 4: Selecting with the Quick Selection Tool

Goal: Isolate an object using **Quick Selection**

Use the Quick Selection Tool to highlight a background.

Refine the edge with "Select and Mask" to smooth the selection.

Replace the background with a new image or solid color.

☑ *What you've practiced:* Smart selections and masking.

📝 Exercise 5: Cropping and Straightening

Goal: Use the **Crop Tool**

Open a slightly tilted image.

Use the Crop Tool and straighten it using the angle line.

Apply the crop and export it.

☑ *What you've practiced:* Crop adjustments and photo correction.

🎨 Exercise 6: Painting and Erasing

Goal: Use **Brush and Eraser Tools**

Create a new layer.

Select a soft brush and paint a light gradient across the canvas.

Use the Eraser Tool with different hardness settings to remove parts of it.

☑ *What you've practiced:* Layered painting and erasing techniques.

⟋ Exercise 7: Creating a Color Gradient Background

Goal: Use the **Gradient Tool**

Create a new document.

Apply a gradient from blue to purple diagonally across the canvas.

Add a circular gradient in the center using Radial Gradient Mode.

☑ *What you've practiced:* Customizing gradients.

🔤 Exercise 8: Adding Text and Shapes

Goal: Use **Text and Shape Tools**

Use the Text Tool to write your name in a bold font.

Add a shape underneath (like a rectangle or custom banner).

Change colors, stroke, or apply effects via the Properties panel.

☑ *What you've practiced:* Combining text and vector shapes in a layout.

Chapter 3: Working with Layers

Layers are the foundation of every Photoshop project. Think of them like transparent sheets stacked on top of one another—each holding a different part of your image. Understanding how to work with them gives you total creative control.

Understanding Layers & Layer Masks

What is a Layer?

A **layer** is an individual level in a Photoshop file that holds a single element—an image, text, shape, or adjustment. You can move, edit, hide, or delete each layer without affecting the others.

Example: A flyer design might have one layer for the background, another for a logo, and separate layers for text and icons.

Types of Layers

- **Image Layers**: Regular pixel-based images.
- **Text Layers**: Created using the Type tool.
- **Adjustment Layers**: Non-destructive edits like brightness, hue, etc.
- **Fill Layers**: Solid colors, gradients, or patterns.

What is a Layer Mask?

A **Layer Mask** allows you to hide or reveal parts of a layer *without permanently erasing anything.* It's a non-destructive way to edit.

- **White** on a mask = reveals the layer
- **Black** = hides the layer
- **Gray** = partial transparency

🗨 **Use Case**: Use a soft black brush on a layer mask to gradually fade an image into the background.

🔧 **How to Add a Layer Mask:**

1. Select your layer.
2. Click the **Add Layer Mask** button at the bottom of the Layers panel.
3. Paint with black or white to control visibility.

Layer Groups and Smart Objects

Layer Groups

Layer groups help you stay organized, especially when working on complex projects with many elements.

- To create a group: Select multiple layers, then press **Ctrl + G / Cmd + G**.
- You can name the group (e.g., "Header Section" or "Icons") for easier navigation.

- Groups can also have their own masks and effects.

🗨 **Use Case**: Group all text layers in a social media post layout to manage them as one.

Smart Objects

A **Smart Object** is a special kind of layer that preserves the original content, no matter how many times you resize or transform it.

Key Benefits:

- Non-destructive editing
- Scalable without losing quality
- Filters applied to smart objects can be edited or removed anytime

🛠 How to Convert a Layer to a Smart Object:

- Right-click the layer > **Convert to Smart Object**

🧠 **Use Case**: You resize a logo multiple times while designing a brochure. Making it a Smart Object prevents distortion.

Blending Modes and Opacity

Blending Modes

Blending modes control how a layer interacts with the layers below it. They're found at the top of the Layers panel (default is "Normal").

Mode	Description
Multiply	Darkens the image by multiplying color values
Screen	Lightens the image by inverting and multiplying

Mode	Description
Overlay	Combines Multiply and Screen for contrast effects
Soft Light	Gentle contrast and color blending
Color	Applies color while preserving brightness from the layer below

💬 **Use Case**: Use Overlay mode to add texture or light effects without hiding the base image.

Opacity and Fill

- **Opacity**: Controls the transparency of the entire layer (0% = invisible, 100% = fully visible).
- **Fill**: Similar to opacity but doesn't affect layer styles (e.g., shadows, strokes).

Example: Lower the Opacity of a photo layer to blend it softly into the background, or reduce Fill while keeping a drop shadow fully visible.

Practice Exercises:

Exercise 1: Stack and Organize

Goal: Understand basic layering

Create a document with 3 images.

Place each on a separate layer.

Rearrange their order and rename them (e.g., Background, Foreground, Overlay).

☑ *You've practiced:* Layer stacking and naming.

Exercise 2: Use a Layer Mask

Goal: Non-destructive hiding

Add a photo to your canvas.

Apply a Layer Mask.

Use a black brush to hide half of the image.

Switch to white to bring parts back.

☑ *You've practiced:* Basic layer masking.

🎁 Exercise 3: Smart Object Scaling

Goal: Resize without quality loss

Import a logo or shape.

Convert it to a Smart Object.

Resize it smaller, then scale it back up.

Observe the clarity difference vs. a rasterized version.

☑ *You've practiced:* Using Smart Objects.

🧺 Exercise 4: Create a Layer Group

Goal: Organize layers

Add text, a shape, and an icon.

Group them into a folder called "Header Elements."

Hide or lock the group to test control.

☑ *You've practiced:* Layer organization.

🎨 Exercise 5: Explore Blending Modes

Goal: See how blending changes layer interaction

Place a grunge texture over a photo.

Cycle through blending modes like Multiply, Overlay, and Soft Light.

Adjust Opacity for subtle effects.

☑ *You've practiced:* Using blending creatively.

Chapter 4: Color and Image Adjustments

Photoshop offers powerful tools to control color and tone—whether you're making a photo pop, correcting a dull image, or stylizing your design for creative impact.

Working with Color Modes

Color modes define how colors are represented and displayed in your project. Choosing the correct mode is essential for print and digital projects.

Common Color Modes

Mode	Description	Use Case
RGB (Red, Green, Blue)	Screen-based colors	Web design, social media graphics

Mode	Description	Use Case
CMYK (Cyan, Magenta, Yellow, Black)	Print-based colors	Posters, brochures, business cards
Grayscale	Shades of gray, no color	Artistic edits, monochrome prints
Lab Color	Based on human vision perception	Advanced color editing

🗨 **Tip**: For digital work, always stick with **RGB**. For print, convert to **CMYK** before exporting.

To change color mode: Image > Mode > [Choose Mode]

⚠ **Note**: Some filters and tools are unavailable in CMYK or Grayscale modes.

Adjusting Brightness, Contrast, Hue, and Saturation

These are basic yet essential adjustments that can dramatically improve an image's appearance.

Brightness/Contrast

- **Brightness** affects overall lightness or darkness.

- **Contrast** affects the difference between light and dark areas.

Access via: **Image > Adjustments >** Brightness/Contrast

🗨 *Use Case*: Fixing underexposed or flat-looking photos.

Hue/Saturation

- **Hue** shifts the overall color tone (e.g., turning blue to green).

- **Saturation** controls the intensity of color (low = muted, high = vibrant).

- **Lightness** affects brightness without changing contrast.

Access via: **Image > Adjustments > Hue/Saturation**

🗨 *Use Case*: Making skies bluer, lips redder, or desaturating for a cinematic look.

Using Adjustment Layers

Adjustment layers are **non-destructive**, meaning they don't permanently change your image. You can edit or remove them at any time.

Common Adjustment Layers:

- **Brightness/Contrast**

- **Levels** – Fine-tunes shadows, midtones, and highlights

- **Curves** – Provides precise tonal control

- **Hue/Saturation**

- **Color Balance** – Adjusts shadows, midtones, highlights separately

- **Black & White** – Converts color to grayscale with full control

Add via: **Layer > New Adjustment Layer** or use the **Adjustment panel**

💬 **Bonus Tip**: Use clipping masks with adjustment layers to apply the effect only to

a specific layer (Right-click the adjustment >
Create Clipping Mask).

Black and White Conversions

There's more to black and white than simply
removing color. Photoshop gives full control
over how each color translates to gray,
making your image more dramatic or
balanced.

Methods to Convert to Black & White:

1. **Black & White Adjustment Layer** – Best
   method

   o Customize how reds, blues, and
      other colors appear in grayscale.

   o Option to tint with color (e.g.,
      sepia tone).

2. **Desaturate** *(Image > Adjustments > Desaturate)* – Fast but lacks control.

3. **Convert to Grayscale Mode** – Permanent and non-editable. Use with caution.

🧠 *Use Case*: Turning portraits into moody, high-contrast black and white images.

Practice Exercises

🔬 Exercise 1: Fix a Dark Photo

Goal: Use Brightness/Contrast

Open a photo with poor lighting.

Apply a Brightness/Contrast adjustment layer.

Tweak settings until the image looks well-lit but natural.

☑ *You've practiced:* Correcting exposure.

Exercise 2: Modify Color Intensity

Goal: Use Hue/Saturation

Open a landscape photo.

Increase saturation to make colors vivid.

Change the Hue slightly to shift the color palette.

☑ *You've practiced:* Enhancing vibrance and exploring color tones.

Exercise 3: Targeted Adjustments with Curves

Goal: Use Curves Adjustment Layer

Add a Curves layer.

Create an S-shaped curve to boost contrast.

Observe how highlights and shadows change in real time.

☑ *You've practiced:* Tonal correction using advanced tools.

🖼 Exercise 4: Convert a Portrait to Black & White

Goal: Use Black & White Adjustment Layer

Open a color portrait.

Add a Black & White layer and adjust each color slider.

Tint the image with a soft brown tone.

☑ *You've practiced:* Non-destructive black and white conversion with creative control.

📎 Exercise 5: Clipping Mask Application

Goal: Use Clipping Masks with Adjustment Layers

Place a photo over a background.

Add a Hue/Saturation adjustment layer.

Right-click > Create Clipping Mask to apply it only to the photo.

☑ *You've practiced:* Isolating adjustments to specific layers.

Chapter 5: Photo Editing & Retouching

Retouching is the art of refining a photo without making it look unnatural. Whether you're removing a blemish, sculpting light with dodge and burn, or using Photoshop's powerful AI tools, these techniques can turn a good image into a polished masterpiece.

Removing Blemishes and Objects

Photoshop offers several **content-aware tools** that make spot corrections almost effortless.

Spot Healing Brush Tool (J)

- Automatically samples surrounding pixels to fix blemishes, dust, and small distractions.

- Works great on skin, fabric, and backgrounds.

🗨 *Use Case*: Instantly remove a pimple or wrinkle from a portrait.

Healing Brush Tool

- Similar to Spot Healing, but you choose the source area manually by Alt-clicking.
- Offers more control for complex textures.

🧠 *Use Case*: Fixing skin with fine textures like pores or makeup.

Patch Tool

- Lets you select an area to replace and drag it over a clean region.
- Best for removing larger objects or patterns (e.g., wrinkles, wires).

Found under the same tool group as Spot Healing (hold-click the icon to access all).

Frequency Separation (Advanced Skin Retouching)

Frequency Separation is a technique used to separate **texture** from **color/tone** so you can edit each independently.

How It Works:

- The **low-frequency layer** contains color and smooth areas.
- The **high-frequency layer** contains fine details like pores or hair.

This allows for skin smoothing *without* blurring natural textures.

💬 *Use Case*: Even out skin tone and correct blotchiness without affecting facial details.

⚠ This technique requires duplicating layers, applying filters (Gaussian Blur, High

Pass), and using brushes or mixers. Best suited for intermediate users.

Dodge and Burn Techniques

Dodging lightens areas, while **burning** darkens them. Together, they sculpt the image to add depth, contrast, and emphasis.

Tools:

- **Dodge Tool (O):** Lightens highlights, midtones, or shadows.
- **Burn Tool (O):** Darkens selected tones.

💬 *Use Case:* Brighten under-eye areas or define cheekbones in a portrait.

Non-Destructive Dodge & Burn:

1. Create a new layer filled with **50% gray**.

2. Set the layer blend mode to **Overlay**.

3. Use a soft brush with low opacity (white = dodge, black = burn).

AI-Based Features (Generative Fill, Neural Filters, etc.)

Photoshop 2025 has pushed the boundaries with powerful **AI enhancements** that save time and unleash creativity.

Generative Fill

- Powered by Adobe Firefly, this feature lets you add, remove, or extend image content using text prompts.
- Works seamlessly with selections.

💬 *Use Case:* Select the sky and type "sunset with clouds" to replace it instantly.

Available via **Right-click > Generative Fill** after making a selection.

Neural Filters

- AI-powered filters for tasks like skin smoothing, colorization, facial expression changes, and depth-of-field simulation.
- Most can be applied with one click and adjusted non-destructively.

To access:

Filter > Neural Filters

Popular options include:

- **Skin Smoothing**
- **Smart Portrait**
- **Style Transfer**
- **Photo Restoration**

Use Case: Smooth skin, change age or gaze direction in a portrait, or restore old photos.

Practice Exercises

◎ Exercise 1: Spot Healing Cleanup

Goal: Remove minor blemishes

Open a portrait photo.

Use the Spot Healing Brush to remove 3–5 blemishes or distractions.

Zoom in to verify blending quality.

☑ *You've practiced:* Quick retouching with content-aware tools.

✂ Exercise 2: Remove an Object with Patch Tool

Goal: Remove larger elements

Select an unwanted object (e.g., wire or logo).

Drag the selection over a clean background area with the Patch Tool.

☑ *You've practiced:* Clean object removal with texture matching.

✏ Exercise 3: Perform Frequency Separation

Goal: Advanced skin retouching

Duplicate your portrait layer twice.

Apply Gaussian Blur to one (low frequency) and High Pass to the other (high frequency).

Use a soft brush or mixer brush to even out tone while preserving texture.

☑ *You've practiced:* Layer-based skin editing.

◯ Exercise 4: Lighten and Darken with Dodge & Burn

Goal: Add depth and structure

Create a 50% gray overlay layer.

Use the Dodge Tool to brighten eyes or forehead.

Use the Burn Tool to add shadow to jawline or hair edges.

☑ *You've practiced:* Manual light sculpting.

🤖 Exercise 5: Use Generative Fill

Goal: Enhance or replace part of an image

Select the sky or a background element.

Open the **Generative Fill** menu and enter a creative prompt (e.g., "city skyline at night").

Choose from AI-generated options.

☑ *You've practiced:* AI-assisted image replacement.

Exercise 6: Apply a Neural Filter

Goal: Use AI to improve a portrait

Open **Filter > Neural Filters**

Enable **Skin Smoothing** or **Smart Portrait**

Tweak the sliders and observe the before/after effect.

☑ *You've practiced:* One-click intelligent adjustments.

Chapter 6: Selections & Masking

In Photoshop, *selections* and *masks* are essential tools for precise editing. They allow you to isolate specific areas of an image to apply changes—without affecting the rest of the picture. Whether you're cutting out a subject, swapping backgrounds, or blending multiple images into one, selections and masks give you pixel-level control over what's visible and editable.

Making Accurate Selections

Photoshop offers a wide range of selection tools. Each is suited for different types of tasks. The goal of making a selection is to isolate part of the image so you can edit, copy, delete, or apply effects to just that area.

- **Key Selection Tools:**

Tool	Best Used For
Rectangular/Elliptical Marquee Tool	Selecting geometric shapes (boxes, circles)
Lasso Tool	Freehand selections with manual precision
Polygonal Lasso Tool	Selecting objects with straight edges

Tool	Best Used For
Magnetic Lasso Tool	Selecting objects with well-defined edges
Quick Selection Tool (W)	Smart brush that expands selection as you drag
Object Selection Tool *(Photoshop 2025)*	AI-powered; auto-detects and selects objects with one click

✎ ***How to Make a Basic Selection:***

1. Select the tool (e.g., Quick Selection Tool).
2. Click and drag over the object.

3. Photoshop will automatically snap the selection to edges.

4. Use shift to add to the selection, or Alt/Option to subtract.

5. Press Ctrl+J / Cmd+J to copy the selection to a new layer if needed.

🧠 **Tip**: Use a soft edge (feathered selection) for blending, and a hard edge when you need precision.

The Select and Mask Workspace

Select and Mask is a dedicated workspace for refining your selections. It's especially useful for tricky areas like hair, fur, or semi-transparent fabrics.

◆ **Accessing It:**

- After making a selection, go to **Select > Select and Mask**
- Or click **Select and Mask** in the top toolbar when using a selection tool

◆ **Main Features:**

- **View Modes**: See your selection over black, white, transparent, or original backgrounds
- **Refine Edge Brush**: Paint around edges (like hair) to let Photoshop refine the selection automatically
- **Global Refinements**:
  ○ **Smooth** – Softens jagged edges
  ○ **Feather** – Softens the selection boundary
  ○ **Contrast** – Sharpens the edge
  ○ **Shift Edge** – Expands or contracts the selection

- **Output To**: Choose whether to apply the selection as a mask, a new layer, or a new file

🗨 **Pro Tip**: Use "On Black" or "On White" views when working with hair—it shows missed edges and halos clearly.

Hair and Edge Refinement

Selecting hair used to be tedious—especially against complex backgrounds. Photoshop 2025 has made it easier with enhanced AI tools.

◆ **Steps to Select Hair Accurately:**

1. Use **Object Selection Tool** or **Quick Selection Tool** to make an initial subject selection.
2. Click **Select and Mask**.

3. In the right panel, click **"Refine Hair"**.

4. Use the **Refine Edge Brush Tool** to manually clean up areas around the hairline.

5. Tweak **Feather**, **Contrast**, and **Shift Edge** to soften or sharpen the transition.

6. Output the result as a **Layer Mask**.

Why Layer Mask? Because it's non-destructive—you can edit the visibility of the cutout without permanently deleting anything.

Compositing Techniques

Compositing means combining multiple images to create one seamless design. This could be placing a model into a new background or combining objects into a surreal scene. Clean selections and masks are the foundation of believable composites.

◆ **Steps for a Simple Composite:**

1. **Open two images** (e.g., a portrait and a landscape background).
2. **Select the subject** from the portrait using Object Selection.
3. **Refine the selection** using Select and Mask.
4. **Output to a Layer Mask** and drag the subject into the new background.
5. **Match lighting and color** using adjustment layers (Curves, Color Balance, or Match Color).
6. **Add shadows** using a soft black brush on a new layer set to **Multiply**.

💬 **Blending Tip**: Use a subtle blur (Filter > Blur > Gaussian Blur) on the masked edges to soften the transition and avoid harsh cutouts.

Practice Exercises

Exercise 1: Select a Simple Object

Goal: Master basic selection tools

Open an image of a clear object (e.g., cup, ball, or logo).

Use the **Object Selection Tool** to isolate the object.

Move it to a blank canvas.

☑ *What you've practiced*: Object-based AI selection

Exercise 2: Select a Subject with Hair

Goal: Use Select and Mask

Open a portrait with flyaway hair.

Use the **Quick Selection Tool** to select the subject.

Open **Select and Mask**, click **Refine Hair**, and use the **Refine Edge Brush Tool** to clean up.

☑ *What you've practiced*: Hair selection and soft edges

Exercise 3: Create a Basic Composite

Goal: Combine two images naturally

Cut out a subject and place them into a new background.

Match the lighting using **Curves** or **Color Balance**.

Add a soft shadow under the subject using a new layer + soft brush.

☑ *What you've practiced:* Compositing with light and realism

---

Exercise 4: Manual Masking for Blending

Goal: Custom mask painting

Add a Layer Mask to any photo.

Use a soft black brush to hide parts of the image.

Switch to white to bring them back gradually.

☑ *What you've practiced:* Hands-on blending with masks

Chapter 7: Filters, Effects, and Styles

Photoshop isn't just for photo corrections—it's also a powerful engine for creative transformation. Whether you're stylizing images, adding dramatic effects, or giving text and objects a unique flair, **filters, effects, and layer styles** help you elevate your design beyond the basics.

Using Built-in Filters

Filters apply predefined effects to an image or selection. Photoshop includes a vast library of built-in filters for creating textures, distortions, stylized looks, and more.

◆ **How to Access Filters:**

- Go to the **top menu** and click **Filter**
- Filters are grouped under categories like:
  - **Blur** (Gaussian Blur, Lens Blur)
  - **Distort** (Twirl, Ripple, Wave)
  - **Noise** (Add Noise, Dust & Scratches)
  - **Sharpen** (Unsharp Mask, Smart Sharpen)
  - **Stylize** (Emboss, Oil Paint)
  - **Render** (Clouds, Lens Flare)

◆ **Popular Filters Explained:**

Filter	Use Case
Gaussian Blur	Softens images or blends edges (great for background blur)

Filter	Use Case
Smart Sharpen	Enhances detail and clarity
Oil Paint	Gives images a stylized, painterly look
Lens Flare	Adds lighting effects for dramatic impact
Emboss	Creates a 3D-engraved texture effect

Tip: Always apply filters to **Smart Objects** for non-destructive editing—you'll be able to tweak or remove them at any time.

Creating Custom Effects

Beyond built-in filters, you can combine tools, blending modes, brushes, and overlays to build **custom effects** like:

- Glows
- Color grading
- Vintage/film looks
- Double exposures
- Light leaks

◆ **Example: Creating a Soft Glow Effect**

1. Duplicate your image layer.
2. Apply **Gaussian Blur** (Radius: 10–20).
3. Change the duplicated layer's **blending mode** to **Soft Light** or **Screen**.
4. Adjust the **opacity** for a subtle or strong glow.

◆ **Other Techniques for Custom Effects**

- Use **Gradient Maps** to apply color effects.
- Combine **Layer Masks + Brushes** to blend multiple images.
- Add overlays (like dust, fog, or light textures) and set them to **Overlay** or **Multiply** blending modes.

🧠 **Pro Tip**: Save your effect layers as **Presets or Actions** so you can apply them quickly to future projects.

Applying Layer Styles

Layer styles are quick, pre-built effects applied to any layer (text, shape, or image). These include shadows, glows, bevels, strokes, and more.

◆ **How to Apply Layer Styles:**

- Right-click a layer > **Blending Options**
- Or click the **"fx" icon** at the bottom of the Layers panel

◆ **Common Layer Styles:**

Style	Description
Drop Shadow	Adds a shadow behind the object—helps create depth
Outer Glow / Inner Glow	Adds a soft colored light around or inside the object
Bevel & Emboss	Gives a 3D-raised or chiseled look
Stroke	Adds an outline around the object (customizable thickness and color)

Style	Description
Gradient Overlay	Fills the layer with a gradient effect

🗨 **Use Case**: Use **Stroke + Drop Shadow** to make text pop over busy backgrounds, or apply **Bevel & Emboss** to give buttons a tactile feel.

Practice Exercises

⚬ Exercise 1: Apply a Stylized Filter

Goal: Use a built-in filter

Open a portrait or photo.

Convert it to a **Smart Object.**

Go to **Filter > Stylize > Oil Paint** or **Filter > Blur > Gaussian Blur.**

Adjust the settings and view the result.

☑ *You've practiced:* Non-destructive filter application.

⚡ Exercise 2: Create a Glow Effect

Goal: Use custom techniques

Duplicate a photo layer.

Apply **Gaussian Blur.**

Change blend mode to **Screen** or **Soft Light.**

Lower opacity as needed.

☑ *You've practiced:* Layer blending for visual effects.

✎ Exercise 3: Build a Custom Light Leak

Goal: Use overlays and blending modes

Import a light leak or gradient overlay.

Set the layer's blending mode to **Overlay** or **Lighten**.

Use a soft brush + mask to blend edges.

☑ *You've practiced:* Creative effect building.

Exercise 4: Use Layer Styles on Text

Goal: Style text like a graphic element

Create a text layer with your name or phrase.

Apply **Drop Shadow**, **Stroke**, and **Gradient Overlay** via **Blending Options**.

Save the style as a preset if desired.

☑ *You've practiced:* Customizing layer appearance with instant effects.

Chapter 8: Working with Text & Design Projects

Photoshop isn't just for photos—it's also a full design platform. From typography to layout, this chapter gives you the tools and confidence to create eye-catching posters, social media graphics, and other visual content that communicates clearly and professionally.

Typography Tools & Tricks

Text is more than just words—it's a design element. Photoshop's text tools help you control not just what's said, but how it feels.

- **Basic Text Tool (T)**

- Click anywhere on the canvas to start typing.
- Use the **Options Bar** at the top to set:
    - Font type
    - Size
    - Color
    - Alignment
    - Style (bold, italic, etc.)

Tip: Hold **Shift** + **drag** to scale text proportionally when resizing.

- **Paragraph vs. Point Text**

- **Point Text**: Click and type—ideal for headlines or short labels.
- **Paragraph Text**: Click and drag to create a text box—best for longer text

or descriptions. Text wraps within the box.

◆ **Character and Paragraph Panels**

Found under **Window > Character** and **Window > Paragraph**

Tool	Use Case
Tracking	Adjusts spacing between all letters
Kerning	Adjusts spacing between two specific letters
Leading	Adjusts line spacing
All Caps / Small Caps	Stylize text with uppercase variations

Tool	Use Case
Justify / Align	Controls paragraph flow (left, center, right, full justification)

🧠 *Pro Tip*: Combine text with **blending modes, layer styles, and clipping masks** to create creative text effects like metallic, cut-out, or image-filled typography.

Creating Posters, Flyers, and Social Media Graphics

Photoshop allows you to design with intention, whether for business promotion, event posters, or social media engagement.

- **Steps for a Design Project (e.g., Poster or Social Media Graphic):**

1. **Create a New Document**
   - Use **File > New**
   - Select a preset size:
     - Instagram Post: 1080 x 1080 px
     - Poster (print): 11 x 17 in at 300 DPI
     - Flyer (web): 1280 x 720 px at 72 DPI
2. **Add Background and Images**
   - Use **Photos > Place Embedded** to insert photos.
   - Apply filters or blur if needed to make text stand out.
3. **Add Text Elements**
   - Use clear, legible fonts for body text.
   - Combine bold fonts for titles with clean fonts for details.

4. **Use Alignment Tools**

   - Turn on **View > Snap To > Guides**.

   - Use **Move Tool + Smart Guides** to align elements precisely.

5. **Organize Layers**

   - Rename and group layers (e.g., "Header Text," "Photos," "Icons").

   - Use **Adjustment Layers** to color grade the final composition.

Exporting for Print and Web

Once your design is complete, exporting it correctly ensures it looks sharp wherever it goes.

- **Export for Web (Digital Use)**

  - Use: **File > Export > Export As**

- Format: **JPEG or PNG**
- Resolution: **72 PPI**
- Color Mode: **RGB**
- Transparency: PNG supports it; JPEG does not

💬 *Use PNG for*: Logos, graphics with transparent backgrounds

💬 *Use JPEG for*: Photos and full-color designs

◆ **Export for Print**

- Use: **File > Save As** or **File > Export > Export As**
- Format: **TIFF, PDF, or High-Quality JPEG**
- Resolution: **300 PPI**

- Color Mode: **CMYK**

💬 *Pro Tip*: Check with your print provider for their preferred format and bleed settings (usually 0.125 inches).

Practice Exercises

🖊 Exercise 1: Create a Social Media Post

Goal: Design a promotional Instagram post

Open a new document (1080 x 1080 px, RGB, 72 PPI).

Add a solid or gradient background.

Insert a product image.

Add 2–3 lines of text (headline, subtext, call-to-action).

Apply a drop shadow and stroke to the headline.

☑ *What you've practiced:* Balanced layout and text styling.

📄 Exercise 2: Make a Flyer for an Event

Goal: Design for print

Create a new document (8.5 x 11 inches, 300 PPI, CMYK).

Add a background image.

Create text blocks for the event name, date, location, and contact info.

Use a shape layer or gradient behind the text to improve legibility.

☑ *What you've practiced:* Poster layout and print-safe design.

---

abc Exercise 3: Apply Advanced Typography

Goal: Customize a headline

Type a headline using the Type Tool.

Adjust **tracking**, **leading**, and **kerning** in the Character panel.

Apply a **gradient overlay** and **drop shadow** from Layer Styles.

Use **Convert to Smart Object** and apply **Filter > Blur > Motion Blur** for a stylized look.

☑ *What you've practiced:* Typographic refinement and stylizing text.

Exercise 4: Export for Web and Print

Goal: Learn file prep for different platforms

Export your social media post as **JPEG (72 PPI, RGB)**.

Export your flyer as **PDF (300 PPI, CMYK)**.

☑ *What you've practiced:* Correct export settings for real-world use.

Chapter 9: Automation & Productivity Tips

Whether you're editing hundreds of photos or just trying to speed up your design process, Photoshop offers powerful features to automate tasks and boost productivity. This chapter will walk you through **actions**, **batch processing**, and **keyboard shortcuts** that can dramatically streamline your workflow.

Using Actions

Actions are like macros: they record your steps in Photoshop and let you replay them instantly—perfect for repetitive edits like resizing, watermarking, or applying a signature style.

◆ **How to Create an Action:**

1. Go to **Window > Actions** to open the Actions panel.
2. Click the **+ icon** to create a new action.
3. Name your action and click **Record**.
4. Perform the steps you want to automate (e.g., resize image, apply filter, save).
5. Click the **Stop** button when done.
6. To replay, select the action and click **Play** ▷ .

💬 *Use Case*: Quickly apply a preset logo watermark on multiple images.

Batch Processing

Batch Processing lets you apply an action to an entire folder of images automatically—no need to open each file one-by-one.

◆ **How to Use Batch Processing:**

1. Create and save your action (see above).

2. Go to **File > Automate > Batch**.

3. Choose your action set and action.

4. Select the source folder (where your images are).

5. Choose a destination folder (where results will be saved).

6. Set file naming conventions and click OK.

💬 *Use Case*: Resizing or applying color corrections to 100 product photos in seconds.

⚠ Make sure your action includes a **Save As** step, or the batch may not save files correctly.

Keyboard Shortcuts for Efficiency

Photoshop is packed with shortcuts that speed up every tool and menu command. Learning just a few can save hours over time.

◆ **Essential Keyboard Shortcuts:**

Action	Windows	macOS
Move Tool	V	V

Action	Windows	macOS
Zoom In/Out	Ctrl + / Ctrl -	Cmd + / Cmd -
Fit to Screen	Ctrl + 0	Cmd + 0
Undo	Ctrl + Z	Cmd + Z
Step Backward (Multiple Undos)	Ctrl + Alt + Z	Cmd + Option + Z
Copy / Paste	Ctrl + C / V	Cmd + C / V
New Layer	Ctrl + Shift + N	Cmd + Shift + N
Transform (Resize/Rotate)	Ctrl + T	Cmd + T
Deselect	Ctrl + D	Cmd + D

Action	Windows	macOS
Show/Hide Rulers	Ctrl + R	Cmd + R

- **Tool-Specific Shortcuts:**

Tool	Shortcut
Brush Tool	B
Eraser Tool	E
Crop Tool	C
Lasso Tool	L
Clone Stamp Tool	S
Text Tool	T
Hand Tool (pan)	H or Spacebar (hold)
Eyedropper	I

Tip: Press **Tab** to hide/show all panels—great for uncluttered work.

Practice Exercises

⚙ Exercise 1: Create a Basic Action

Goal: Record and play back a custom action

Open any photo.

Open the **Actions** panel.

Record an action that:

Duplicates the layer

Applies **Gaussian Blur**

Changes the blend mode to **Soft Light**

Stop recording.

Play the action on a new image.

☑ *What you've practiced:* Action creation and re-use.

📁 Exercise 2: Batch Process Multiple Images

Goal: Apply an action to a folder of files

Create an action that resizes an image to 1000px wide.

Save 3–5 sample images in a folder.

Use **File > Automate > Batch** to apply the action to all images.

☑ *What you've practiced:* Folder-wide automation.

⌨ Exercise 3: Use 10 Essential Shortcuts

Goal: Build shortcut muscle memory

Practice the following shortcuts:

Ctrl/Cmd + Z (Undo)

Ctrl/Cmd + D (Deselect)

B (Brush)

T (Text Tool)

V (Move Tool)

Ctrl/Cmd + 0 (Fit to Screen)

Ctrl/Cmd + T (Transform)

Spacebar (Pan)

Ctrl/Cmd + R (Rulers)

Ctrl/Cmd + Shift + N (New Layer)

☑ *What you've practiced:* Fast, efficient Photoshop movement.

Chapter 10: Advanced Techniques

This chapter brings everything together for users ready to elevate their skills beyond the basics. From animation to Camera RAW to non-destructive workflows, these techniques unlock the full potential of Photoshop—especially for creative professionals, content creators, and photographers.

Working with 3D (If Still Supported)

⚠ **Note:** As of Photoshop 2023, Adobe began phasing out 3D features due to performance and compatibility issues. In Photoshop 2025, **native 3D tools are either deprecated or very** limited. Adobe recommends using **Substance 3D apps** for full 3D workflows.

That said, some **3D text and basic extrusion** features may still be accessible through:

- **Filter > 3D > Generate 3D Depth Map** (if enabled)
- **Layer > New 3D Extrusion from Selected Layer** (may be hidden or unsupported)

Workaround: If your version doesn't support 3D, use **layer styles, shadows, and bevel effects** to mimic 3D text or shapes.

Creating Animated GIFs

Photoshop allows simple frame-by-frame animations—perfect for banners, social media GIFs, or looping sequences.

◆ **Steps to Create a Basic Animated GIF:**

1. **Open or create a layered document** (each frame = one layer).
2. Go to **Window > Timeline** to open the animation timeline.
3. Click **Create Frame Animation**.
4. Click the menu icon > **Make Frames from Layers**.
5. Set **frame delay time** for each frame.
6. Choose **Forever** in looping options.
7. Preview with the play button.

◆ **Export as GIF:**

- Go to **File > Export > Save for Web (Legacy)**.
- Choose **GIF** format.
- Set looping to **Forever**, and click **Save**.

Use Case: Create a 4-frame text reveal animation for Instagram Stories or email marketing.

Non-Destructive Editing

Non-destructive editing means making changes to your image without permanently altering the original pixels. This allows you to go back, re-edit, or remove effects at any time.

 Best Practices for Non-Destructive Workflows:

Technique	Description
Smart Objects	Convert layers to Smart Objects to preserve original data and allow re-editable filters
Adjustment Layers	Apply color and tonal changes without altering the image directly
Layer Masks	Hide parts of a layer instead of erasing them
Clipping Masks	Apply effects to specific layers only
Blend If (Layer Style)	Control layer visibility based on brightness without masks

Tip: Never use the **Eraser Tool** directly on an original image—mask it instead!

Working with Camera RAW

Camera RAW is an essential tool for photographers, allowing high-level editing of RAW image files with greater precision and quality retention.

- **How to Access Camera RAW:**

  - Open a RAW file (e.g., .CR2, .NEF, .ARW) and Photoshop will automatically launch **Adobe Camera RAW (ACR)**.
  - You can also apply Camera RAW to non-RAW images via:
    Filter > Camera Raw Filter

- **Main Features in Camera RAW:**

Panel	What It Does
Basic	Adjust exposure, contrast, highlights, shadows, whites, blacks
Tone Curve	Fine-tune brightness and contrast
Color Mixer	Adjust hue, saturation, and luminance by color
Detail	Sharpening and noise reduction
Effects	Add grain, vignettes
Calibration	Color profile tweaks for advanced users

🧠 *Use Case:* Fix an underexposed photo, remove color casts, or give your photo a cinematic color grade.

Practice Exercises

🌀 Exercise 1: Create a Simple Animated GIF

Goal: Make a looping animation

Create 3–5 text layers with slightly different content (e.g., "Sale Starts Now" > "Up to 50% Off" > "Shop Today!").

Open the **Timeline** and make frames from layers.

Set frame delay to 0.5s and loop forever.

Export as a GIF using **Save for Web**.

☑ *You've practiced:* Frame animation and web export.

💡 Exercise 2: Apply Non-Destructive Filters

Goal: Use Smart Objects and masks

Import a photo.

Convert it to a **Smart Object**.

Apply **Gaussian Blur** via **Filter**.

Use a **layer mask** to reveal only parts of the blur (e.g., a shallow depth-of-field effect).

☑ *You've practiced:* Layer protection and mask-based edits.

📷 Exercise 3: Edit a RAW File with Camera RAW

Goal: Enhance photo quality

Open a RAW file or apply the **Camera Raw Filter** to a JPEG.

Adjust **Exposure**, **Contrast**, **Whites/Blacks**, and **Texture**.

Export the photo or open it into Photoshop for further editing.

☑ *You've practiced:* Professional-level photo enhancements.

🧊 Exercise 4: Simulate 3D Text

Goal: Use layer styles to mimic 3D

Create a bold headline using the **Text Tool**.

Apply **Bevel & Emboss**, **Drop Shadow**, and **Gradient Overlay**.

Adjust depth and shadow angle for a 3D illusion.

☑ *You've practiced:* Styling text without true 3D features.

Bonus Section

Common Mistakes and How to Avoid Them

Even experienced users fall into traps that lead to frustration or poor results. Recognizing these pitfalls can save time, prevent errors, and produce cleaner work.

◆ **Mistake 1: Editing on the Background Layer**

Why it's a problem: Any edits made directly on the background layer are permanent and destructive.

☑ **What to do instead**: Always duplicate the background layer (Ctrl/Cmd + J) or convert it to a **Smart Object** before making changes.

◆ **Mistake 2: Overusing Filters or Effects**

Why it's a problem: Too many filters, glows, or shadows can make designs look amateurish or dated.

☑ **What to do instead**: Use effects *sparingly and purposefully*. Ask, *"Does this enhance or distract from the message?"*

◆ **Mistake 3: Ignoring Resolution and Color Settings**

Why it's a problem: Wrong resolution (e.g., 72 PPI for print) or wrong color mode (RGB for print) leads to poor output.

☑ **What to do instead**:

- For **print**: 300 PPI, CMYK
- For **web**: 72 PPI, RGB

◆ **Mistake 4: Flattening Too Early**

Why it's a problem: Flattening merges all layers, making it impossible to adjust elements later.

☑ **What to do instead**: Keep a layered .PSD **version** of your file before flattening or exporting.

---

* **Mistake 5: Using the Eraser Instead of Layer Masks**

Why it's a problem: The Eraser tool permanently removes pixels.

☑ **What to do instead**: Use **Layer Masks** for non-destructive control over visibility.

Real-World Projects to Practice

These mini-projects are designed to help readers apply everything they've learned in realistic, goal-driven scenarios.

Project 1: Design a Promotional Poster for a Local Event

- Create an 11x17" CMYK canvas
- Use images, shape layers, and styled text
- Apply blending modes and layer styles
- Export as print-ready PDF and digital JPG

Project 2: Retouch a Professional Headshot

- Use **Spot Healing Brush, Dodge/Burn,** and **Frequency Separation**
- Apply **Camera RAW Filter** for final tonal control
- Save as web and high-res print versions

🔖 **Project 3: Social Media Brand Pack**

- Create an Instagram post, Facebook banner, and YouTube thumbnail using consistent colors and branding
- Use **Smart Objects** to make reusable templates
- Apply non-destructive edits and save as PSD/PNG

Project 4: Create an Animated Product GIF

- Animate text or icons on a 1080x1080 canvas using the **Timeline**
- Export as a looping GIF for web

Project 5: Composite a Fantasy Scene

- Combine 3–5 images into one surreal landscape
- Use **Select and Mask, Layer Masks,** and **Color Grading**
- Apply finishing effects like **Light Leaks** or **Gradient Maps**

Resource List (Brushes, Plugins, Tutorials)

To keep growing, readers need high-quality, safe, and trusted resources. This curated list points them in the right direction.

Free & Premium Brushes

- **Adobe Brushes Library** – https://www.adobe.com/products/photoshop/brushes.html

- **Brusheezy** – https://www.brusheezy.com *(Free & Premium)*

- **Kyle T. Webster Brushes** *(Included with Adobe Creative Cloud)*

⚡ Popular Plugins

- **Nik Collection** – Powerful photo filters and effects
- **Retouch4Me** – AI-based retouching plugin for portraits
- **ON1 Effects** – One-click presets and filters
- **Infinite Color Panel** – AI-powered color grading for creatives

---

🎓 Tutorial Websites

- **Adobe Help Center** – https://helpx.adobe.com/photoshop/tutorials.html
- **PHLEARN** – https://phlearn.com *(Free & Premium Photoshop courses)*

- **Piximperfect (YouTube)** – Highly detailed, practical Photoshop tutorials
- **Envato Tuts+** – https://tutsplus.com *(Project-based lessons)*